AMPHIBIANS

CREATURES
OF THE
LAND AND WATER

AMPHIBIANS
CREATURES OF THE LAND AND WATER

BY EDWARD J. MARUSKA
Executive Director, Cincinnati Zoo
and Botanical Garden

A Cincinnati Zoo Book
FRANKLIN WATTS
New York • Chicago • London • Toronto • Sydney

FOR ALEXANDRA, CHELSEA, CHRISTOPHER, AND NICHOLAS.
MAY THEY NEVER KNOW A SILENT POND.

Frontis: *Bambina orientalis* (top); *Dendrobates leucomelas* (center);
Pseudoeurycea belli (bottom)

Cover photographs copyright © Cincinnati Zoo/Edward J. Maruska

Photographs copyright © Cincinnati Zoo and: Ron Austing: pp.13
bottom left, 15, 26 right, 29 center; Penny Geary: p. 46; all other
photographs copyright © Cincinnati Zoo/Edward J. Maruska.

Illustration by Allan P. Sutherland

Library of Congress Cataloging-in-Publication Data

Maruska, Edward J.
    Amphibians / by Edward J. Maruska.
        p.   cm. — (A Cincinnati Zoo book)
    Includes bibliographical references and index.
    ISBN 0-531-11158-X (lib. bdg.) — ISBN 0-531-15714-8 (pbk.)
    1. Amphibians — Juvenile literature.   [1. Amphibians.]   I. Title.
    II. Series.
    QL644.2.M3155   1994
    597.6 — dc20   93-29843   CIP   AC

CONTENTS

A NEW CLASS OF ANIMALS

7

TAILLESS AMPHIBIANS: THE ORDER ANURA

19

TAILED AMPHIBIANS: THE ORDER URODELA

31

THE CAECILIANS

47

WHERE HAVE ALL THE AMPHIBIANS GONE?

51

GLOSSARY

61

CONSERVATION ORGANIZATIONS

63

FURTHER READING

63

INDEX

64

A NEW CLASS OF ANIMALS

In the stillness of an ancient swamp about 350 million years ago, a fishlike animal struggled from the murky water onto the land, able to breathe air through its simple lungs. So began an adventure, the settling over the land by the *vertebrate* animals (animals with a backbone). Vertebrates, although not the most numerous members of the animal kingdom, continue to rule the planet. The ancient shallow seas and lakes were filled with many kinds of aquatic vertebrates, but before this time, the only animals successfully living on land were huge dragonflies, cockroaches, and other *invertebrates* (animals without backbones). The early vertebrates who ventured into a new environment were the first of a class of animals that had never existed before on Earth — the *amphibians*.

The word amphibian comes from a Greek word, *amphibios*. *Amphi* means "both," and *bios* means "life." True to this name, most amphibians lead two-part lives — the first part in water and the second at least partly on land. Like their ancestors the fishes, all amphibians are vertebrates, which means they have backbones and internal skeletons.

There are five main groups of vertebrates: fishes, amphibians, reptiles, birds, and mammals. Scientists refer to each of these groups as a class. The fishes are in the Class Pisces, the amphibians

An aquatic salamander, the red-bellied newt, *Taricha rivularis*

in Amphibia, the reptiles in Reptilia, the birds in Aves, and the mammals in the Class Mammalia.

Scientists break each class down into smaller categories called orders, and then into families, genera, and species. We will use only the class, order, and family divisions in our look at amphibians.

Most amphibians are small, backboned animals. They lack scales, feathers, or hair, and the paired fins of fish. Instead of fins, most adult amphibians have four limbs. The front limbs have feet with four toes and the hind feet have five. Many people confuse amphibians with reptiles. But unlike dry-skinned reptiles, amphibians have bare, spongy skin containing glands that produce a slimy substance. This slime coats the skin and protects it from drying out.

Here is the way a scientist might look at and classify a leopard frog:

Kingdom: Animalia (Animal)
Phylum: Chordata (with a backbone)
Class: Amphibia (a double life)
Order: Anura (tailless amphibian)
Family: Ranidae (grass frog, lake frog, and wood frogs)

The two further breakdowns are:
Genus: *Rana*
Species: *Rana pipiens*

The leopard frog, *Rana pipiens* — with light-edged, dark spots that give it its name — is a common amphibian.

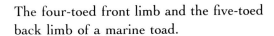

The four-toed front limb and the five-toed back limb of a marine toad.

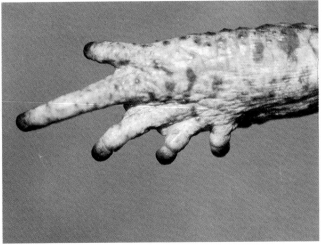

Above: If a creature's skin is dry, like this Gila monster's, it's probably a reptile.
Below: If the skin is slime-covered and moist, like this Colorado River toad's, it's an amphibian.

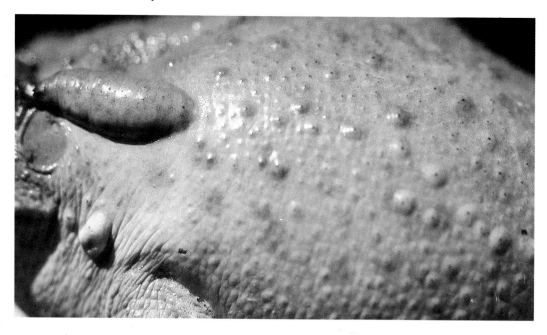

The amphibian class is divided into three basic groups:
Urodela: tailed amhibians, the salamanders
Anura: tailless amphibians, the frogs and toads
Gymnophiona: caecilians, burrowing wormlike amphibians

Above: A palm salamander, *Bolitoglossa platydactyla* (Order: Urodela). Below, left:
A golden mantella, *Mantella aurantica*, a small frog from Madagascar (Order:
Anura). Below, right: A Mexican caecilian, *Dermophis mexicanus*
(Order: Gymnophonia). All are members of the class of animals called amphibians.

FROM EGGS TO ADULTS

The life cycle of most amphibian species begins when females lay masses of jellylike, large-yolked eggs in water. *Embryos* develop inside the eggs and hatch into *larvae*. After many changes, the larvae reach their adult form. A tadpole (the larval stage) looks very different from an adult frog. It has a fat, cigar-shaped body with a tail and no legs. But as it grows, spectacular changes take place. Rear legs appear and, as it continues to feed and grow, front legs sprout from the body. After time, changes begin to occur around the head. The eyes start to bulge out and the tadpole's small, thick-skinned mouth begins to widen. The tail is slowly absorbed into the body, and the froglet begins to breathe through its newly developed lungs, instead of the tadpole gills. Soon it moves onto land. This amazing series of body changes is called *metamorphosis*. The pattern of metamorphosis is somewhat different among various amphibians.

The life cycle of most amphibian species follows a pattern from eggs to embryos to larvae to adults. The photos on this page show (left) a mass of frog eggs; (right) large-yolk salamander eggs.

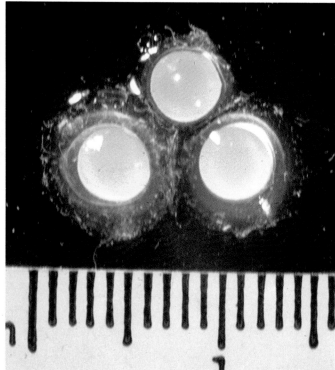

The photos here show the next stages of development. Above: Salamander embryos developing inside eggs. Below, left: Frog larvae (tadpoles). Below, right: A young salamander larva. Adult forms appear on the next page.

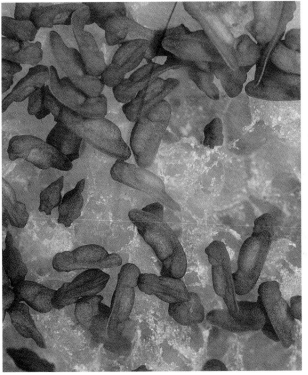

After the process of metamorphosis is complete, the adult animals appear.
Above: An adult Santa Cruz long-toed salamander, *Ambystoma macrodactylum croceum*. Below: An adult Inyo County toad, *Bufo exul*.

Amphibians *fertilize* their eggs in a variety of ways. In most frogs and some salamanders, the male and female mate in the water. The female deposits eggs into the water and the male releases sperm into the water over the freshly laid eggs. Among some salamanders, the male deposits a packet of sperm (a *spermatophore*) in front of the female, often after a fancy courtship display. The female moves over the spermatophore and picks it up with her body and stores it until her internal eggs are ready for fertilization. This method of reproduction allows some kinds of salamanders to live their entire lives on land, away from permanent streams or ponds, laying large-yolked eggs in moist areas. The large yolk of the egg provides food for the developing young. For these salamanders, metamorphosis occurs within the egg. When the young hatch, they are tiny versions of the adult salamander.

Spring peepers, *Hyla crucifer*, and most other frog species, mate in ponds or other wet places.

Some salamanders lay large-yolk eggs in which their young develop. The top photo shows a European cave salamander, *Hydromantes italicus,* in captivity with newly laid eggs. The bottom photo shows tiny Cheat Mountain salamanders, *Plethodon nettingii nettingii,* that hatch from eggs.

Salamanders lack an eardrum and middle ear, and so are deaf to airborne sounds. Thus it is not surprising that salamanders are mostly silent and do not vocalize. Frogs and toads have external ears and males vocalize. They croak to signal their own kind and to attract females to the breeding ponds. In spring, frog and toad choruses are common and create incredible noise in the woods.

Because their skin is thin and naked, amphibians must live in moist areas. They also need moist areas or water to keep their shell-less eggs from drying out. They do not drink, but absorb water through their skin. The skin of many species has special glands that produce poison for protection. They have lungs for breathing but can also breathe through their skin.

Amphibians, like fish and reptiles, are *cold-blooded* animals. Mammals, including humans, make their own body heat and regulate it inside their bodies. However, cold-blooded animals cannot control their body temperatures from within. Some move to a warmer spot, or retreat into the shade to adjust their internal temperatures for survival.

The amphibians' two-part existence has succeeded for millions of years. But, in today's world, their future looks uncertain. The world would be a poorer place without the amphibians, yet their real significance is that they were the first backboned animals to move onto the land, and they provided an evolutionary beginning for all the rest of the land-dwelling vertebrates, including human beings.

Ancestors of this red-eyed tree frog, *Agalychnis callidryas*, were the first vertebrates to move onto the land.

Oriental fire-bellied toad, *Bombina orientalis*

Ringed salamander, *Ambystoma annulatum*, of eastern North America

Asiatic climbing toad, *Pedostibes hosii*

Red Hills salamander, *Phaeognathus hubrichti*, of Alabama

Painted mantella frog, *Mantella madagascariensis*, of Madagascar

Palm salamander, *Bolitoglossa mexicanum*, of Mexico

There are about 2,500 different kinds of amphibians known today. New species are still being found, especially in the rain forests of Africa and South America. Some of the great variety of salamanders and frogs are shown here.

TAILLESS AMPHIBIANS: THE ORDER ANURA

The order Anura is made up of various animals we often call frogs. We can tell them apart from other amphibians by the fact that adults lack tails. They have long hind legs and a short, sturdy backbone that helps them withstand the shock of long leaps on land. These are the most agile of amphibians, able to hop, jump, and leap.

FROGS OR TOADS?

Toads look different from frogs. Most frogs have naked, smooth, moist skin, and are long-limbed and web-footed. They live in, near, or around water. Most kinds of toads, however, have thick skin that looks dry and is usually covered with wartlike glands. These glands can produce poisons that make the animals taste bad to predators. The thick outer skin also allows toads to live in dryer areas, often far from water. Toads usually have short legs, and webless hind feet.

However, it is risky to try to separate frogs from toads just by their looks. As many Anuran families include both "froglike" and "toadlike" species, it is easy to make mistakes. The body shape of what we call a frog or toad has evolved in response to the environment in which it lives. For example, some tree-dwelling frogs have flat bodies that allow them to press close to a tree's leaves or bark

Sometimes it is easy to tell a frog from a toad: (top, left) a thin-skinned tomato frog; (top, right) a thick-skinned Mexican toad. Right: A close-up look at the poison gland (the worm-shaped area to the right of the eye) that makes this Colorado River toad taste bad to its enemies.

so they are disguised while they rest. Some species of tree frogs have sticky pads on their toes that aid them in climbing. Some kinds burrow underground for food and safety. They have pointed heads, and sometimes have sharp ridges along the sides of the head to break through soil. Thus we can't always assign a label of "frog" or "toad." In this book we can safely refer to all as frogs.

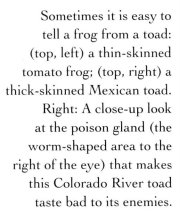

Both amphibians, this tree frog, *Phyllomedusa trinitatis* (top photo) and burrowing frog, *Rhinophyrnus dorsalis* (lower photo) have body characteristics that help them survive in very different habitats.

FROG SENSES

Like all amphibians, frogs are cold-blooded. Their body temperature is about the same as the outside temperature. To regulate their body temperature they seek sun to warm up or shade to cool

Basking in the sun will help raise the body temperature of this Zetek's frog, *Atelopus varius zeteki*, to that of the surrounding air.

off. In northern areas, when the temperature begins to drop too low, the frog populations become sluggish and burrow into the pond mud. They enter a deep sleep, or torpor. When the air and water temperatures rise, they become active again. In hot areas frogs may burrow underground and sleep until cooling rains come. This behavior varies from species to species. Some kinds can survive in a wide variety of conditions and flourish in many different habitats and climates, while others can tolerate only small temperature changes.

A frog's head emerges right from the body, with no neck in between. Its bulging eyes and nostrils are on top of the head. This enables the animal to breathe and to see while sitting in water or hidden among plants. Many frogs have long sticky tongues that they flick out to catch insects.

The upper part of the frog's eyeball is shielded by a thick, immovable layer of skin. The lower part is protected by a clear membrane that moves up to cover the eye. To swallow food, frogs close their eyelids, which presses in their eyeballs. This action, along with some help from their tongues, forces the food down into their gullets.

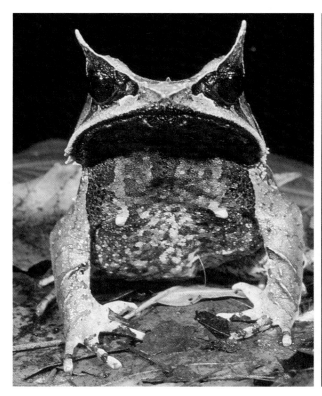

Above: Two of the world's interesting frog species: The Malayan leaf frog, *Megophrys monticola* (left) has excellent camouflage. The broken outline created by its eye crests and its leaflike colors help it blend into the litter on the forest floor. The casque-headed tree frog, *Triprion spatulatus* (right) hides in the hollows of trees and uses its unusually shaped head to block the entrance.

Below: A close-up look at a spiny-headed tree frog, *Anotheca spinosa* (left) shows the eyes and nostrils. The photo of the American bullfrog, *Rana catesbeiana* (right) shows the tympanum, or external eardrum.

Among amphibians, only the frogs have developed vocal chords and a larynx, or voice box. A male frog inflates its throat sac and pumps air in and out to produce a loud croak. The early frogs' croaking sounds echoing through ancient forests were the first vocal communication among land vertebrates. Frogs also have eardrums, which receive sound waves from the air. The eardrums are large, conspicuous discs located behind the eyes in many species. A covering of skin, called the tympanic membrane, protects them.

With vocal sac inflated, this male American toad, *Bufo americanus*, can produce sounds to attract mates or scare away rivals.

THE FROG LIFE CYCLE

Frogs are generally found in or near water. Nearly all frog species need water for mating and laying their eggs — a pond or stream, or even a low area where a puddle regularly forms. When they mature, some frogs move away from their hatching place, in search of a food supply with fewer competing frogs around. But in the

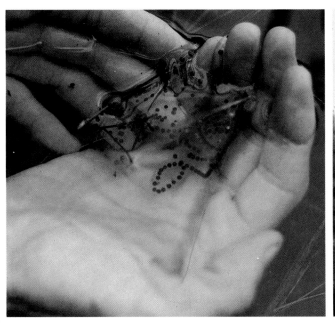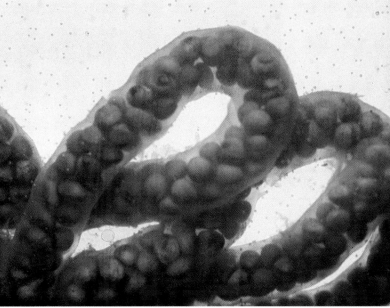

Left: A mass of Houston toad eggs. Right: A magnified view of toad eggs.

spring, or when the weather is favorable, such as during heavy rains, frogs travel back to their breeding sites. Males begin croaking and, as more and more collect at the site, the frog chorus builds to an almost deafening level. The chorus can be heard for miles around, and attracts great numbers of male and female frogs to *spawn*. Some species assemble by the hundreds of thousands — if the breeding site has not been polluted or destroyed.

Frogs lay their eggs in a mass, which varies in size from one kind of frog to another. So, too, does the water temperature where the eggs are laid. Egg masses of frogs that spawn in cold water have a globular or round shape and are attached to an underwater branch or plant. An egg mass spawned in warmer water will film out over the surface. (Warmer water is poorer in oxygen. If the egg mass spreads out, each developing tadpole will have a better chance of getting sufficient oxygen.) Several frog species build foam nests for their eggs either on or near water. The females whip up secretions from their bodies. These harden in the air and provide a protective coating that keeps the eggs from drying out. Often many females work together, beating the secretions in the water until very large foam nests are formed to hold thousands of developing eggs.

Depending on the species, frogs may deposit from as few as 6 to as many as 20,000 eggs. The tadpole or larval form does not look like the adult at all. Tadpoles have short, spherical bodies with broad, rudderlike tails. At this stage of their development, they have a *lateral line system* that includes sensory cells that respond to pressure changes and vibrations in the water.

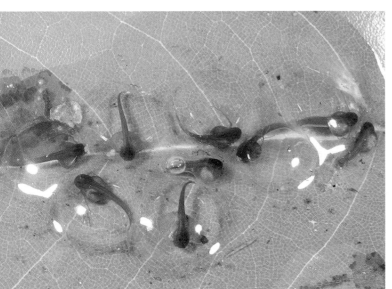 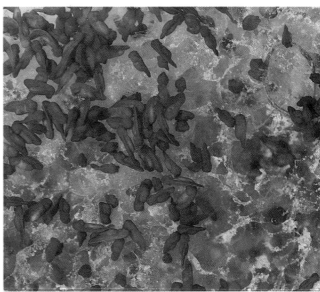

Left: Inside their own jellylike eggs, these arrow poison frog tadpoles are nearly ready to hatch. Right: A just-hatched group of leopard frog tadpoles.

Most tadpoles are *herbivorous*; they feed on various aquatic plants, including *algae*. They have a large gut to hold the plant food that they eat. The mouthparts of tadpoles vary from species to species according to how they eat—whether they graze on plants, or *siphon* up food particles from the surface of the water. A few kinds of frog tadpoles are *carnivorous*, and feed on any species of aquatic life they can overpower, including other tadpoles.

As the tadpole changes to a frog, its lungs develop, its legs begin to appear, and its tail is slowly absorbed into the body. Complete development from tadpole to frog may take as little as two weeks for some temporary pool breeders. But the bullfrog, and some others, may spend several seasons in the larval form.

The tadpole's tail is absorbed,
and finally a frog appears.

A few species of frogs, like the greenhouse frog, lay a small number of eggs on land. Each larva develops within its egg capsule and the young hatch as fully developed froglets — tiny copies of their parents. Some other species have *brood chambers*, either in the throat or in the folds in the skin of the back, where the eggs develop.

The Surinam toad's method of breeding is very unusual. During an elaborate underwater courtship the male, in a graceful motion, fertilizes each newly laid egg and then deposits it on the spongy back of the female. The eggs develop in individual pockets in the skin. After a period of development, the young pop out of the skin of the female's back as miniature versions of the adult toad.

Tailless amphibians include some 3,500 species. They range from the Arctic Circle to deserts and savannahs, and into tropical rain forests and up to mountain tops. This great number of frog species, and their wide distribution over the Earth, are evidence of the order's success in adapting to the environment. Whether they continue to be successful and survive may depend on how we human beings help preserve their homes.

The Surinam toad, *Pipa pipa* (below, left) breeds in an unusual way. As the female deposits eggs, the male fertilizes them and maneuvers them onto the female's back (below, right), until as many as 60 eggs are in place (opposite page, top). The eggs are gradually absorbed into pits in the spongy skin (center). After incubation, the pits pop open and tiny Surinam froglets appear (bottom).

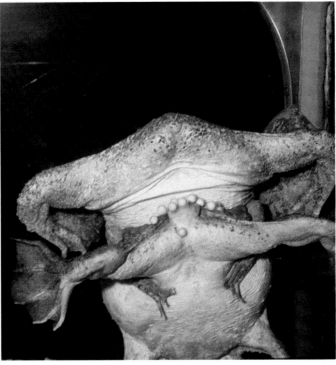

It may be hard to tell a salamander (above) from a lizard (below) when they're scurrying out of sight. But a closer look shows many differences.

TAILED AMPHIBIANS: THE ORDER URODELA

Urodela, the second order of amphibians, is made up of over 300 species of salamanders. These amphibians keep their tails through their life cycle.

Salamanders are very secretive animals that usually scurry into hiding when people approach. People who manage to see them often confuse them with lizards. But a careful observer can find many clues to tell them apart. Lizards have dry, scaly skin; salamanders have naked, moist skin. Lizards thrive in dry, hot areas, while salamanders must seek cooler, humid areas for survival. Lizards have ear openings, while salamanders are nearly silent animals and have no external ear openings. They detect approaching danger by picking up vibrations through their front feet or through their jawbones. Lizards have five clawed toes on each foot, while most salamanders have four clawless toes on their forelimbs.

The word salamander comes from an ancient Greek word meaning "fire animal." In early times, when people carried firewood into their homes, they often brought along salamanders that were hiding among the moist logs. As the logs were placed on the fire, the salamanders sensed the heat and scurried from the hearth. The people imagined the animals were "born of fire" and could survive the flames.

Salamander species cover a wide variety of sizes: from the largest of all living amphibians, the 4.5-foot (1.37-meter) giant salamander of China and Japan, to the tiny, under 2-inch (5-centimeter) pygmy salamander of North America's Smoky Mountains.

The giant salamander of Asia, *Andrias japonicus* (left) is 27 times the size of the pygmy salamander of North Carolina, *Desmognathus aeneus* (right).

LAND AND WATER CREATURES

As amphibians, many salamanders spend part of their lives in water and part on land. The tiger salamander, and the spotted and spring salamander spend their juvenile life in the water and then undergo metamorphosis. They lose their gills and leave the water to live the adult phase of their lives on land. In contrast, some species of salamander (among them the siren, mud puppy, and Texas blind salamander) live a wholly aquatic life. A third group, terrestrial, or land-living, salamanders, spend their entire lives on land, often far from large, permanent bodies of water. These ground dwellers lay eggs with larger yolks than those of the aquatic forms. Offspring develop through the juvenile larva stage within

Tiger salamander, *Ambystoma tigrinum*

Turkish brook newt, *Neuergus crocatus*

Spring salamander, *Gyrinophilus porphyriticus*

the egg capsule. The eggs hatch on land and the young emerge looking like miniature adults. All woodland salamanders, such as the slimy and red-backed salamanders, reproduce in this manner. Many tropical salamanders, such as the palm salamanders, also lay eggs on land. The European alpine salamander holds its developing eggs within its body and gives birth to fully formed young.

The Corsican brook salamander, *Euproctus montanus* (above) lays eggs in water to produce a new generation. The Okinawan spiny newt, *Tylototriton andersoni* (below) lays eggs on land. They eventually hatch tiny copies of the adults.

Like all other amphibians, salamanders develop from eggs that have been fertilized with sperm from the male. In some salamander species, eggs and sperm are just deposited in a pond (as with fish). Water currents bring them together for fertilization. This is called external fertilization, or fertilization outside of the animal's body. Other salamander species follow long, elaborate courtship routines after which the male deposits a *spermatophore*, the cone-shaped capsule containing sperm. The female follows and picks up the capsule with a special body opening, the *cloaca*, and stores it inside her body. In this method, fertilization is internal, or inside the body. With this method of reproduction, some species were able to move fully onto land. They developed a terrestrial form of life, away from a water source. These amphibians could deposit eggs on land because water was not needed to mix sperm and egg.

Left: This photograph offers a rare view of a slimy salamander, *Plethodon glutinosus*, depositing eggs. Right: Even in captivity, a slimy salamander coils around its newly laid eggs.

In both aquatic and amphibious species, when the young hatch they have tiny, external gills so they can breathe in water. If we look closely, we can see three separate rows of gills on each side of the head. The gills are well supplied with blood vessels and so look reddish. Salamanders that live in still ponds or stagnant water have larger and fuller gills than those of species living in free-running, oxygen-rich streams or rivers. Fuller gills offer a greater surface to fill the salamanders' oxygen needs in the oxygen-poor water.

This small-gilled Tennessee cave salamander, *Gyrinophilus palleucus* (left) lives in oxygen-rich water, while the larger-gilled tiger salamander larva, *Ambystoma tigrinum* (right) lives in oxygen-poor water.

Soon after hatching, the larva develop leg buds and, before long, four legs sprout from them. The tail is broad and rudderlike and helps the young propel themselves through the water. The larva's lateral line organs show (under magnification) as small spots in regular rows along its head, back, and sides. Each spot shows a depression that contains a hairlike sensor bristle that is connected to nerve endings. These organs sense vibrations in the water and help the larval salamander find food or escape from enemies.

Salamander larvae have wide mouths, equipped with many teeth. They are carnivorous, and will eat almost any animal life

Above, left: Leg buds are beginning to appear on this newly hatched Texas blind salamander, *Typhlomolge rathbuni*, larva. Right: After about eighteen weeks, the larva has well-developed legs. Below: The lateral line sense organs can be seen above and below the eye of this Mexican ambystoma larva.

available, including smaller salamanders. Because of this characteristic, salamander larvae are more solitary than plant-eating frog tadpoles.

After eating and growing for a period of time the larva begins to prepare to leave the water. Gills shrink and the lateral lines disappear. The tail becomes less broad and more round. In many species a striking color change occurs. Once its lungs are well developed, the young salamander crawls from the water and seeks shelter under a rock or log, or burrows into the soil. It is now an adult salamander. The next breeding season it will return to its breeding grounds, along with hundreds of other salamanders, to reproduce.

Some salamander species do not complete the transformation from larva to adults. They reach sexual maturity during the larval stage. The axolotol that lives in lakes around Mexico City is an example. The salamanders breed while in the gilled stage and rarely transform to the adult phase. This occurs mostly in hot, dry areas where life for adult-phase animals is difficult.

The axolotol

Generally, salamanders lay their eggs and then desert them. However, the giant salamanders of Asia and North America, and some other species, give more parental care. Several females deposit fertilized eggs in a common nest. A male guards them until they hatch. The females of many terrestrial lungless salamanders "guard" their eggs by staying near them through development. Their moist skin protects the eggs from drying out, and secretions from their skin may guard against fungus growth on the eggs.

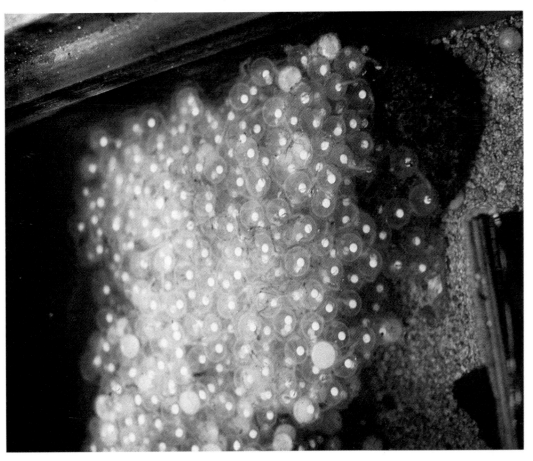

Nearly hidden behind a huge communal nest, a male giant salamander guards the eggs.

Adult salamanders have long bodies with long tails and two sets of paired limbs (except for the siren, which lacks hind legs). They breathe through lungs and through their skin. The skin is always moist and is richly supplied with blood vessels for an easy transfer of gases. Through evolutionary changes, some species of salamanders have completely lost their lungs and breathe only through their skin and the inner surface of their mouths.

An adult spotted salamander, *Ambystoma maculatum* (above) and (below) a lesser siren, *Siren intermedia*, with no hind limbs

A number of mammals, birds, reptiles, and amphibians find sala-manders tempting food. To ward off enemies, many species have poison glands in their skin that produce substances to discourage predators. Sometimes bold, bright colors warn of their poisonous skin. Other salamanders, like the slimy salamander, when threat-ened produce a milky-looking, sticky solution all over their bodies. This *mucus* makes them an unpleasant prospect for a meal. If this protection fails, a salamander may shed its tail. The wiggling tail distracts the predator long enough for the salamander to escape. If a predator bites off a salamander's tail, the salamander can scurry off, leaving the tail behind in its enemy's mouth. In time, the salamander grows a new tail.

Many amphibians have a trace of poison in their skins. Among the arrow poison, or poison dart, family of frogs, skin glands produce poisons strong enough to protect them from would-be predators. Their bright colors may serve to warn these enemies of the poison. Below: the red and black arrow poison frog, *Dendrobates histrionicus* (left) and the blue dart frog, *Dendrobates azureus*. Other species appear on the following page.

Above: The granular arrow poison frog, *Dendrobates granuliferus*; Below, left: The yellow-banded arrow poison frog, *Dendrobates leucomelas*; Below, right: The three-striped dart frog, *Epipedobattes trivittatus*.

Some salamanders have adapted to unusual environments. Strange cave-dwelling types spend their entire lives in an unchanging darkness. These aquatic, deep-cave dwellers lack the skin color of their surface relatives. The olm of the Balkan region and the Texas blind salamander from caves in Central Texas are examples. They look white or pinkish, with red gills behind their heads. They are sightless, and depend on vibrations and touch to locate food. We do not know much about the life cycles of deep-cave salamanders as their *habitats* are so difficult to reach.

The Cincinnati Zoo, working with the Texas Department of Wildlife, has acquired some specimens of the Texas blind salamander to try to learn more about these ghostly creatures. The Zoo succeeded in getting them to mate and produce eggs and the eggs were successfully hatched. This was the first time the eggs and newly hatched young of this species were described for science.

To learn about the strange cave-dwelling salamanders, scientists set out to explore their habitat and acquire specimens for study.

Above: The ghostly Texas blind salamander, *Typhlomolge rathbuni*. Below: The salamander with newly laid eggs, in captivity. This was the first time the eggs of this species were ever seen and recorded.

Because salamanders are secretive, we can study them only in captivity. We are not sure how long salamanders live in the wild, but we see that the specimens being studied at the Cincinnati Zoo laboratories live long lives. Some specimens of delicate salamanders have lived in the Zoo's collections for twenty-five years. A giant salamander at the Amsterdam Aquarium lived for over fifty years.

Besides being secretive, salamanders also come out only at night, when conditions are favorable. The rest of the time they hide under leaves or logs or burrow into the soil. The best time to look for them is with a flashlight on a rainy night in the spring. If you are lucky enough to spot one moving about in the shadows, perhaps on its way to its breeding pond or seeking a meal, do not disturb it. You can watch it and, if possible, record its behavior, because you probably won't see another one until the next spring—the most active time for tailed amphibians.

The giant salamander can grow to a length of more than 4 feet.

Tropical rain forests offer the warm moist climate and abundant insect life
that caecilians thrive on.

THE CAECILIANS

The third order of amphibians are the mysterious caecilians (sah-SEAL-ee-uns) that we still know little about. These wormlike burrowing animals live in tropical areas of Central and South America, Asia, and Africa. There are about 160 species. A few species are wholly aquatic and spend their lives in sluggish rivers.

The first time I held one of these wriggling creatures in my hand I found it difficult to hold, and just as difficult to believe I was looking at a cousin to frogs and salamanders. If you look at a frog and a salamander side by side, you can see a relationship between them. But the creature I was holding, with its long, limbless body marked by segmented rings, looked more like a fat worm than like any amphibian I had ever seen. When I looked closely at the end that was trying to push through my fingers, I could make out tiny, skin-covered eyes, a well-defined mouth and nostrils, which at second glance took it out of the category of wormlike invertebrates and placed it as a vertebrate, or backboned animal — a caecilian. As the small, angular head burrowed between my fingers, I noticed small, active feelers, or tentacles, between its eyes and nostrils. These feelers help the animal to detect odors. When I inspected its open mouth with a magnifying glass, I saw rows of hooked teeth on the upper and lower jaws.

A slimy, hard-to-hold caecilian, *Dermophis mexicanus*

Since caecilians burrow in the soil and spend most of their time underground, they are among the least-known animals. They live in warm, moist soil with abundant leaf litter. The caecilians live in subtropical and tropical Central and South America, Asia, Africa, and some islands in the Indian Ocean. Earthworms, termites, and soft-bodied insects seem to be their preferred food. Some kinds are specialized to feed only on termites. Fertilization is internal for caecelians, and at least half the species lay eggs. The female deposits up to two dozen eggs in a hole or burrow near the edge of a stream. To protect the eggs, the female remains coiled about them until they hatch. Newly hatched larvae have paired external gills and wriggle into the streams, where they stay until they metamorphose into adults.

In other species, females retain their eggs in their bodies for development, nourishing the young with secretions, or "milk," from internal glands. The young are born alive as miniature adults. All aquatic caecilians bear live young. Some species of caecilians are totally aquatic and are often mistaken for fish.

Caecilains are rarely seen or photographed. This picture of a yellow striped caecilian of Thailand, *Icthyophis kohtaoensis*, shows the animal's ringed body and the sensory tentacles, which help it detect odors.

Some kinds of caecilians have mucus glands in their skin that protect them from snakes and birds, their primary enemies. When the animal is disturbed, these glands produce sticky secretions all over the body. Some kinds also have poison glands that produce a substance harmful to predators.

Unfortunately, it is not likely that many readers will see live specimens of these wormlike, nearly blind amphibians. They live only in the tropical parts of the world and, even in their native countries, they are rarely seen because of their burrowing habits. Occasionally children in the tropics uncover one, but they seldom realize that the wriggling creature is not a worm.

A polluted environment can lead to more frequent mutations, such as seen in this six-legged bullfrog.

WHERE HAVE ALL THE AMPHIBIANS GONE?

"Boys throw stones at frogs in sport,
the frogs do not die in sport,
but in earnest."

Bion

Today many amphibian species are declining or vanishing altogether. Zoologists, scientists who study animals, have been reporting gradual losses in amphibian populations for the past twenty-five years. The losses are now rapid and alarming, and scientists are working hard to find reasons for the decline.

Many amphibians face great threats to their habitats as people cut down forests and drain swamps and other wetlands for development. Poison sprays used to kill insects that harm food crops also threaten amphibian survival. Many of these insect poisons are deadly to amphibians worldwide.

Scientists believe there are a number of different reasons for the decline in amphibian populations and the loss of species. Not all agree on which factor is the most harmful. However, they do agree that human industrial activities are responsible.

Amphibians are especially sensitive to pollution and human misuse of the environment. We consider them land vertebrates; however, they inhabit wet or damp places. Because of their moist skin, poisons caused by industrial pollution can pass easily into their bodies. Their delicate skin absorbs insect poisons, detergents, and other industrial wastes. To survive their enemies, some frog species deposit large numbers of eggs — sometimes tens of thousands by one female — and all may be lost to water pollution. Their moist, thin skins and life in water and on land make amphibians more vulnerable when land or water, or both, are damaged by pollution in a natural area.

In years past, coal miners feared exposure to deadly, odorless gases when working in a mine. Mine operators would carry a canary into the mine shaft as a test to see if such gases were

A spoiled habitat causes diseases in salamanders and other vulnerable amphibians.

present. If the canary lived, the mine was safe. Like the canaries that died while providing a warning of harmful gases deep in coal mines, amphibians may be giving us an early warning signal, showing by their decline the presence of poisons in our world.

Amphibians also suffer from acid rain and snow that result when wastes are released into the air through the burning of fossil fuels (coal and oil). Acid rains fall into the ponds and lakes, causing high levels of acid that can harm fragile frog and salamander eggs.

Amphibians that live at high mountain altitudes also are disappearing at an alarming rate, even though their habitats are still

healthy. Scientists are concerned that the greenhouse effect, or the destruction of the protective layer of ozone by pollution in the atmosphere, may be the problem. They fear that holes in this protective layer may allow harmful rays of sun to penetrate. Tests have shown that these harmful rays may damage the eggs of mountain-living frogs and salamanders.

Amphibians with limited habitats are threatened by the loss of breeding ponds due to construction of houses, factories, and other buildings. The massive cutting down of trees worldwide may be causing slight changes in climate and may lead to a warmer and drier earth — certainly not a good place for most amphibians.

Amphibians also face the problem of the introduction of non-native game fish into the lakes and streams where amphibians live or breed. These predatory fish can quickly consume all the frogs and salamanders that never had to cope with large fish, and so have developed no defenses against them. And despite the poisonous or unpleasant substances frogs produce to discourage animal predators, human predators find frogs increasingly appealing. Ten times more frog legs are now eaten than twenty years ago. The United States, Belgium, France, and Italy import tons of frog legs every year. Each ton accounts for about 20,000 frogs.

This Lake Patzcuaro salamander, *Ambystoma dumerilii*, began to disappear when an aggressive game fish, the black bass from North America, was introduced into its Mexican habitat.

Amphibians occur from south of the Equator to the Arctic Circle. During 1990, scientists found declining populations in North America, Central and South America, Europe, Asia, Africa, and Australia. So we are losing many frogs, toads, and salamanders.

Does it really matter that the amphibian world is shrinking? You cannot destroy large parts of a natural system without causing large changes in everything else. Suffering populations of amphibians have led to silent ponds, rivers, mountains, and rain forests throughout the world.

Amphibians occur in enormous numbers, and are building blocks in all natural systems. They are important in the flow of food energy because they eat insects and are eaten by other animals. India used to export large numbers of frog legs for food to

Many tropical salamanders, such as this palm salamander from Central America, *Bolitoglossa subpalmata*, feed on insects, which helps keep animal species in balance.

Europe and North America. Then India found it had to deal with a reduced frog population and plagues of harmful insects. Frogs were discovered to be a cheap, safe way of controlling harmful insects.

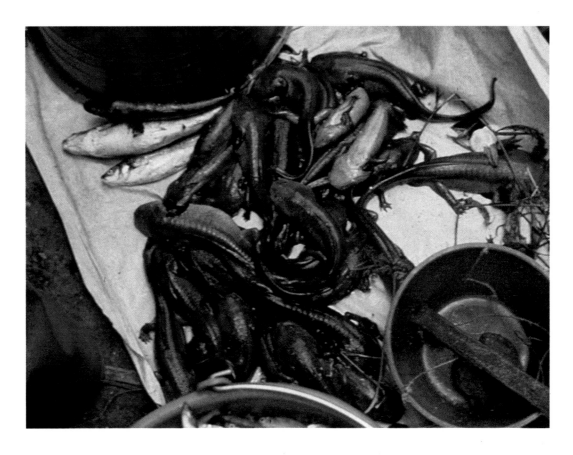

Amphibians, such as these salamanders, and fish are sold as food in markets around Lake Patzcuaro.

Development, loss of wetlands, forest burning and cutting continue to reduce amphibian habitats. High levels of air- and water-borne pollutants harm remaining areas. The disappearance of amphibians may be a warning of a worldwide problem threatening all living animals, including us.

Today a variety of recovery efforts are under way to help save threatened amphibians. Highly endangered species, such as the Houston toad and the Puerto Rican crested toad, are being bred in cooperative efforts at North American zoos, and are being

To help endangered species survive, North American zoos have created breeding programs. In Texas, eggs of the endangered Houston toad are collected at a breeding pond. The eggs are hatched in the zoo, and the young toads are raised there before being released into their natural habitat.

This adult Houston toad, *Bufo houstonensis*, is the product of the successful breeding program at the Houston zoo.

successfully reestablished in the wild. Habitat preservation is vital for the survival of many species, and the United States Fish and Wildlife Service is working to protect wetland and forest habitats for species like the red hill salamander and other endangered amphibians.

Amphibians, as a group, have survived on Earth for the past 350 million years. They were the dominant terrestrial vertebrates for over 100 million years. They survived the age of the dinosaurs, the rise of the mammals, and the development of civilization. Through all these changes the amphibians have adapted and survived. Only today, because of more direct human pressures, are the amphibians at risk of disappearing. The first true voice to chirp and croak over the Earth may now be whispering farewell.

Puerto Rican crested toad, *Peltophryne lemur*

Malaysian red-eyed frog, *Leptobrachium hasseltii*

Chinese alligator newt, *Tylototriton verrucosus*

Blackchin red salamander, *Pseudotriton ruber schencki*

Yellow-eyed tree frog, *Agalychnis annae*

GLOSSARY

Algae (AL-jee) — group of chiefly aquatic, free-floating, often single-celled plants (sea-weeds and pond scum are examples of algae). Pond scum is an important food for frog tadpoles.

Amphibian (am-FIB-ee-un) — class of vertebrates; includes salamanders, frogs, toads, and caecilians. Amphibians have two-part lives, spending the juvenile portion in water and the adult on land. They have moist skin, mostly without scales; and two pairs of legs, used in swimming or terrestrial locomotion; up to five toes and hind feet that are often webbed; and breathe through lungs, skin, and lining of the mouth.

Anura (an-yur-A) — one of the three orders of amphibians; consists of the frogs and toads. "Frog" and "toad" are general terms based on superficial appearances and do not necessarily indicate relationship.

Aquatic (ah-KWAH-tic) — any organism, plant or animal, that is adapted to living in or near water.

Caecilians (sah-SEAL-ee-uns) — legless tropical or subtropical aquatic or burrowing worm-like amphibians.

Carnivorous (kar-NIV-uh-rus) — feeding on animal flesh.

Cloaca (clo-AY-cuh) — a body opening through which the intestinal, urinary, and reproductive ducts discharge their contents.

Cold-blooded — any animal that regulates its body temperature chiefly by means of outside sources of heat or cooling.

Embryo (EM-bree-oh) — animal in the early stages of development, either in an external egg or within the body.

Fertilization — union of male sperm and female egg to form a fertilized egg.

Gymnophiona (jim-no-FEE-on-a) — order of tropical wormlike amphibian species without legs. Their skin has glands that secrete an irritating fluid. A small tentacle can be seen between the eye and nostril.

Habitat (HAB-i-tat) — the particular area and physical conditions where an animal or plant lives.

Herbivorous (her-BIV-uh-rus) — relying on only plant food for survival.

Invertebrates (in-VER-tuh-brates) — animals without vertebrae columns, or backbones.

Larva (LAR-vah) — the first stage of a metamorphosing species of amphibian. Larvae have special organs like fins and webbed feet, that may change in the adult stage, and a body shape necessary for an aquatic existence.

Lateral Line System — a network of nerve centers over the head and body of larval salamanders as well as most fish.

Mucus (MYOO-kus) — a sticky, slimy protective secretion produced by mucus glands in the skin. In terrestrial amphibians, it provides protection from drying out. In many amphibians, the mucus has a poisonous or irritating effect to would-be predators.

Metamorphosis (met-uh-MORE-fah-sis) — physical change or transformation as, for example, from juvenile tadpole to adult frog.

Siphon feeding — some frog tadpoles have a wide developed mouth on the top of their heads. This allows for a continuous flow of surface water into their mouths. Specialized mouthparts allow them to draw off, or siphon, food floating at the surface.

Spawn — to release eggs or sperm from the body, usually directly into water. A method of reproduction used by most fish, frogs, and some primitive salamanders.

Species (SPEE-sheez) — a group of plants or animals of the same kind. Members of the same species can mate and produce young with each other.

Spermatophore (spurm-AT-oh-for) — a gelatinous mass consisting of a cone of jelly with a sperm cap on top; deposited by male salamanders during courtship, and picked up by the cloacal lips of females.

Terrestrial (tuh-RES-tree-uhl) — living in or on land.

Urodela (YUHR-uh-dela) — one of the three orders of amphibians, with a long body shape and a distinct head, trunk, and tail. Many species have grooves on the sides of their bodies (caudal fold). There are generally four weak limbs, and the tail does not disappear after metamorphosis. Larvae have external gills.

Vertebrates (VER-tuh-brates) — animals with backbones.

CONSERVATION ORGANIZATIONS

Center for Reproduction
of Endangered Wildlife
Cincinnati Zoo & Botanical Garden
3400 Vine Street
Cincinnati, OH 45220

Conservation International
1015 18th Street, NW
Suite 1000
Washington, DC 20036

Greenpeace, USA
1436 U Street, NW
Washington, DC 20039

League of Conservation Voters
1150 Connecticut Avenue, NW
Washington, DC 20036

National Wildlife Federation
1400 16th Street, NW
Washington, DC 20036

The Nature Conservancy
1815 N. Lynn Street
Arlington, VA 22209

Rain Forest Action Network
301 Broadway, Suite A
San Francisco, CA 94133

The Sierra Club
730 Polk Street
San Francisco, CA 94109

The Wilderness Society
900 17th Street, NW
Washington, DC 20036

Wildlife Conservation International
NYZS/The Wildlife Conservation Society
185th Street & Southern Blvd.
Bronx, NY 10460

Wildlife Preservation Trust International
34th Street & Girard Avenue
Philadelphia, PA 19104

World Wildlife Fund
1250 24th Street, NW
Washington, DC 20037

FURTHER READING

Capula, Massimo. *Reptiles and Amphibians of the World*. New York: Simon and Schuster, 1989.

Conant, R., and J. T. Collins. *A Field Guide to Reptiles and Amphibians of Eastern and Central North America*. Boston: Houghton Mifflin Co., 1991.

Downer, Ann. *Spring Pool: A Guide to the Ecology of Temporary Ponds*. New York: Franklin Watts, 1992.

Duellman, W. E., and Linda Trueb. *Biology of Amphibians*. New York: McGraw-Hill, 1986.

Grzimek's Animal Life Encyclopedia. Vol. 5. New York: Van Nostrand Reinhold, 1970.

Smith, H. M., *A Guide to Field Identification: Amphibians of North America*. New York: Golden Press, 1978.

Smyth, H. R., *Amphibians and Their Ways*. New York: Macmillan, 1968.

Zim, H. S., and H. M. Smith. *Reptiles and Amphibians: A Guide to Familiar American Species*. New York: Simon and Schuster, 1953.

INDEX

Page numbers in *italics* refer to illustrations.

Ambystoma, Mexican, *37*
Amphibians:
  classes of, 8, 10
  decline of, 51–57
  in food chain, 54–55, *55*
Anura, 10, 19–28
Axolotol, *58*

Body temperatures, 17, 21–22
Bullfrogs, 23, *50*

Caecilians, 10, *11*, 47–49, *48*
  Mexican, *11*
  yellow striped, *49*
Camouflage, *23*

Diseases, *52*

Ears, 16, *23*
Egg-laying, eggs, 12, *16*, 23–28, *25*, *26*, *29*, 32, 34, *35*, *39*, *44*, 51–52, *56*
Eyes, 22, *23*

Feeding, 26, 36, 38
Frogs, 19–28
  adult, *14*
  arrow poison, *41*, *42*
  burrowing, *21*
  dart, *41*, *42*
  leopard, *9*
  Malayan leaf, *23*
  Malaysian red-eyed, *58*
  painted mantella, *18*
  red-eyed tree frog, *17*
  spring peepers, *15*
  tomato, *20*
  Zetek's, *22*

Gila monster, *10*
Gills, 36
Golden mantella, *11*

Greenhouse effect, 53
Gymnophiona, 10

Habitat, 32–34, 43, *46*, 48, 51–53, 55

Invertebrates, 7

Larvae, 12, *13*, 36–38, *36*, *37*, 48
Life cycle, 12, *12–13*, 23–28, 32–39, 48
Lizards, *30*, 31

Metamorphosis, 12, 12–14, 15, 26, 27, 32–34
Mucus, 41, 49
Mutations, *50*

Newts:
  Chinese alligator, *59*
  Okinawan spiny, *34*
  red-bellied, *8*
  Turkish brook newt, *33*

Poison glands, *20*, 49
Pollution, 51–52, 55
Predators, 53

Rain forests, *46*
Reproduction, 15, 25–26, *28–29*, 35, 38
  in zoos, 56
Reptiles, 8

Salamanders, 31–45
  adult, *14*
  blind, *44*
  blackchin red, *59*
  cave-dwelling, *36*, *37*, *43*
  Cheat Mountain, *16*
  Corsican brook, *34*
  European cave, *16*
  giant, *32*, *39*, *45*
  Lake Patzcuaro, *53*

vs. lizards, *30*, 31
  palm, *11*, *18*, *54*
  pygmy, *32*
  Red Hills, *18*
  ringed, *18*
  Santa Cruz long-toed, *14*
  slimy, *35*
  spotted, *40*
  spring, *33*
  Tennessee cave, *36*
  Texas blind, *37*, *44*
  tiger, *33*, *36*
Senses, 21–23
Sirens, lesser, *40*
Skin, *10*, 17, 51
Spring peepers, *15*
Survival, 41–45, 49, 51–57

Tadpoles, 12, *26*, *27*
Toads, 19–20
  American, *24*
  Asiatic climbing, *18*
  Colorado River, *10*, *20*
  Houston, *56*, *57*
  Inyo County, *14*
  marine, *9*
  Mexican, *20*
  Oriental fire-bellied, *18*
  Puerto Rican crested, *58*
  Surinam, *28–29*
Tree frogs, 20, *21*
  casque-headed, *23*
  red-eyed, *17*
  spiny-headed, *23*
  yellow-eyed, *60*

Urodela, 10, 31–45

Vertebrates, 7–8, 47
Voice, 23

Water, 23, 25, 35